NEIL DIAMOND
FOR UKULELE

Cover photo by Photofest

ISBN 978-1-4234-9642-7

HAL•LEONARD®
CORPORATION

7777 W. BLUEMOUND RD. P.O. BOX 13819 MILWAUKEE, WI 53213

Visit Hal Leonard Online at
www.halleonard.com

America

from the Motion Picture THE JAZZ SINGER
Words and Music by Neil Diamond

Home, to a new and a shin-y place,

make our bed, and we'll say our grace. Free-dom's light burn-ing

warm, free-dom's light burn-ing warm.

Interlude

Chorus

Ev-'ry-where a-round ___ the world, they're com - ing to A -

mer - i - ca. Ev - 'ry time ___ that flag's ___ un - furled, ___

they're com - ing to A - mer - i - ca.   Got a dream to take _

_ them there.   They're com - ing to A - mer - i - ca.

Got a dream _ they've come _ to share.   They're com - ing to A -

Outro

mer - i - ca.   They're com - ing to A - mer - i - ca.

They're com - ing to A - mer - i - ca.   They're com - ing to A -

mer - i - ca.   They're com - ing to A - mer - i - ca _ to - day, _

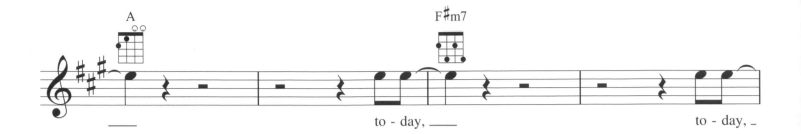

to - day, ____   to - day, _

to - day, ____   to - day. _

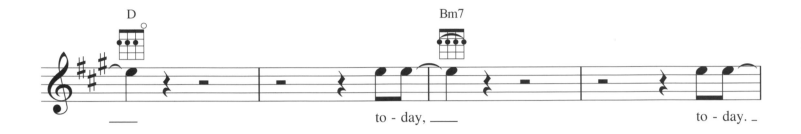

My coun-try 'tis of thee, (To - day,) ____ sweet _ land of

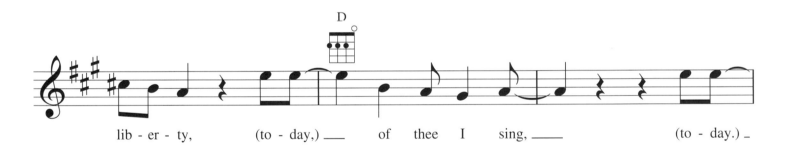

lib - er - ty, (to - day,) ____ of thee I sing, ____ (to - day.) _

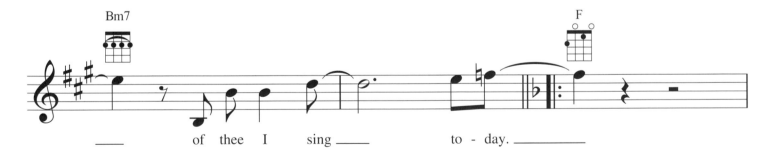

____ of thee I sing ____ to - day. ____

Repeat and fade

To - day, ____   to - day. _

Cracklin' Rosie

Words and Music by Neil Diamond

First note

Verse
Moderately

1. Crack-lin' Ros-ie, get on board. __ We're gon-na ride __ till there ain't __
(D.C.) *Vocal ad lib.*

__ no more __ to go. Tak - in' it slow. __

And, Lord, don't you know I'll have me a time __ with a poor __

__ man's la - dy! 2. Hitch - in' on a twi - light train. __
3. Crack - lin' Ros - ie, make me smile. __ And

Ain't noth-ing here __ that I care __ to take __ a - long, may-be a song __
girl, if it lasts __ for a hour, __ that's __ al - right, 'cause we got all night __

hang on to me,___ girl, our song___ keeps run - nin'   on.___

N.C.(G)

___   Play it now! __   Play it now! __   Play __ it now,

1.   2.   **Verse**

my ba - by!   my ba - by!   4. Crack-lin' Ros - ie, make me   smile. __

___   And, girl, if it lasts _ for an hour, _____ that's al -

right, 'cause we got all night ___   to set the world right. _

D.C. and fade

Dm   G7

___ Find us a dream _ that don't ask ____ no ques - tions.

9

Cherry, Cherry

Words and Music by Neil Diamond

First note

Verse
Brightly

1. Ba - by loves _ me, yes, yes, _ she does.
2. Y'ain't got no _ right, no, no, _ you don't,

Ah, the girl's out - a sight, _ yeah.
ah, to be so ex - cit - ing.

Says she loves _ me,
Won't need bright _ lights,

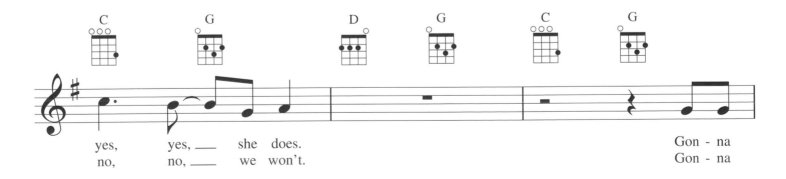

yes, yes, _ she does.
no, no, _ we won't.

Gon - na
Gon - na

Bridge

Tell your ma - ma, girl, __ I can't stay long.
No, we won't __ tell a soul __ where we gone __ to.

We got things __ we got __ to catch
Girl, we do __ what - ev - er we

up on. Ah, you know, __ you know __ what I'm
want to. Ah, I love __ the way __ that you

say - ing. Can't stand still __
do me. Cher - ry, babe, __

__ while the mu - sic is play - ing.
__ you real - ly get to me.

Interlude

2nd time, D.S. and fade

12

Forever in Blue Jeans

Words and Music by Neil Diamond and Richard Bennett

__ by the fire, __ all a - lone _____ you and I; _____

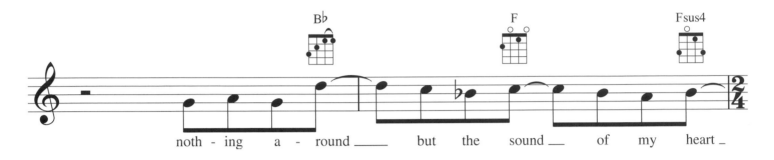

noth - ing a - round _____ but the sound __ of my heart _

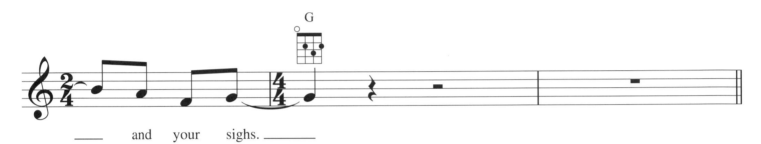

__ and your sighs. _____

Chorus

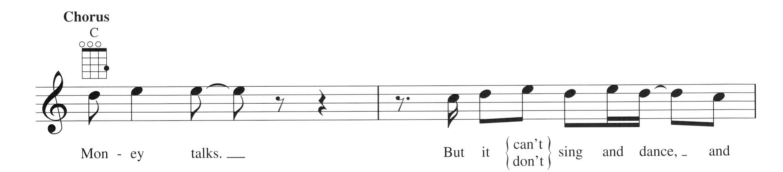

Mon - ey talks. ___ But it ⎰can't⎱ sing and dance, _ and
⎱don't⎰

it ⎰can't⎱ walk. ___ And long as I can have you
⎱don't⎰

here with me, ____ I'd much rath - er be ____ for - ev - er in

blue jeans, babe. __ Hon-ey's sweet. __

But it ain't noth-ing next to ba-by's treat. __

And if you par-don me, I'd like to say ___ we

D.S. al Coda

do o - kay ___ for-ev-er in blue jeans.

⊕ **Coda**

Outro

blue jeans, babe. __ And if you par-don me, I'd
blue jeans, babe. __ And long as I can have you

Repeat and fade

like to say ___ we do o - kay ___ for-ev-er in
here with me, ___ I'd much rath-er be ___ for-ev-er in

Heartlight

Words and Music by Neil Diamond, Burt Bacharach and Carole Bayer Sager

young boy's   dream. ____   Don't wake me   up   too   soon. __

To Coda

Gon-na take   a   ride   a - cross   the   moon, __

you   and   me. ____

D.S. al Coda

Coda

3. He's look - in'   for

you   and   me. __

Outro

Turn   on   your   heart - light   now. __

Turn   on   your   heart - light   now.

18

Girl, You'll Be a Woman Soon

Words and Music by Neil Diamond

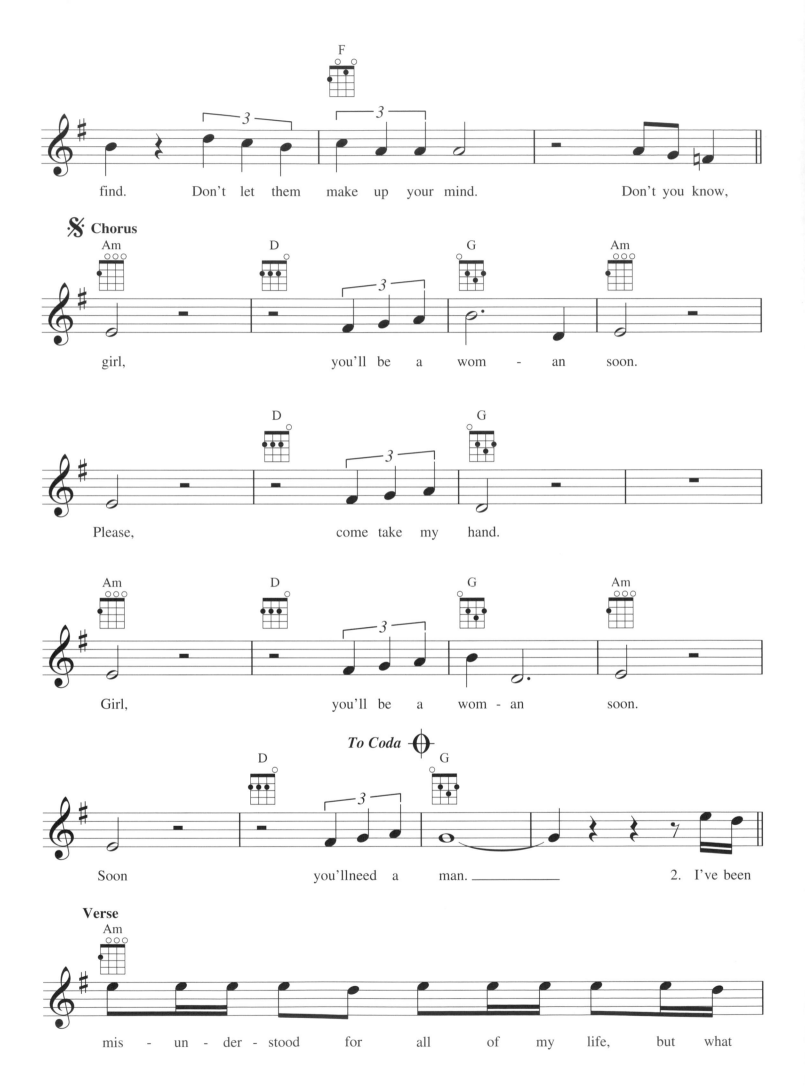

find.   Don't let them   make up   your mind.   Don't you know,

Chorus

girl,   you'll be a   wom - an   soon.

Please,   come take my   hand.

Girl,   you'll be a   wom - an   soon.

To Coda

Soon   you'llneed a   man. _____   2. I've been

Verse

mis - un - der - stood   for   all   of   my life,   but   what

they're say-in', girl, just cuts like a knife: __ "The boy's no good." _

__ Well, I fi-nal-ly found what I've been look-ing for, __ but if

they get the chance they'll end it for sure. _____ Sure they would. _

D.S. al Coda

__ Ba-by, I've done all I could. It's up to you,

Coda

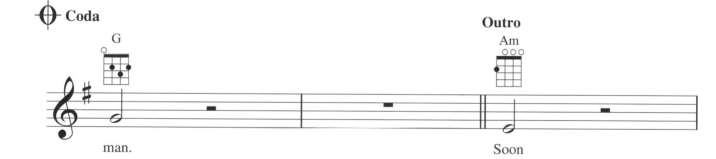

man. Soon

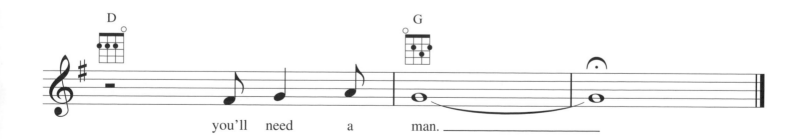

you'll need a man. _____

Hello Again

from the Motion Picture THE JAZZ SINGER
Words by Neil Diamond
Music by Neil Diamond and Alan Lindgren

Holly Holy

Words and Music by Neil Diamond

Bridge

Yeah! Yeah! Call the sun in the dead __

__ of the night, __ oh, the sun __ gon - na rise __ in the sky. __

Touch a man who can't walk __ up - right, __ and that lame __

__ man, he __ gon - na fly. __ And I fly. __

Chorus

To Coda

Yeah! And I fly. __ Hol - ly ho - ly love, __

__ take the lone - ly child. __

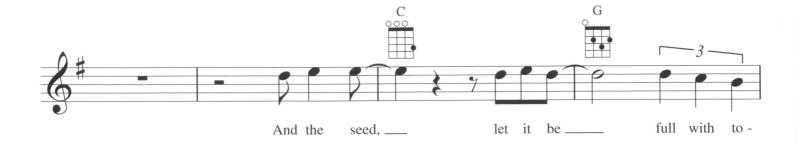

And the seed, ___ let it be ___ full with to-

D.S. al Coda

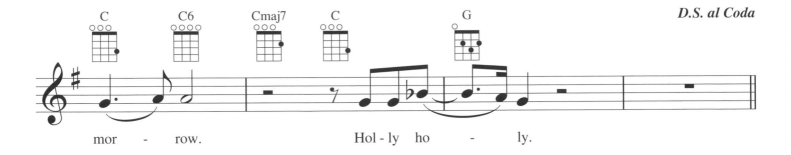

mor - row. Hol - ly ho - ly.

Coda
Outro

Hol - ly ho - ly dream, ___ dream of on-

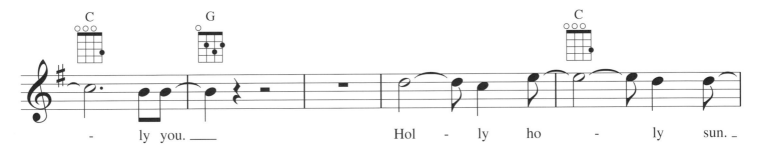

- ly you. ___ Hol - ly ho - ly sun. ___

___ Hol - ly ho - ly rain. ___

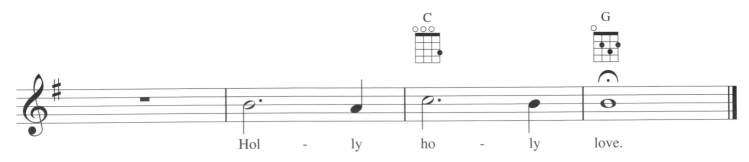

Hol - ly ho - ly love.

I Am...I Said

Words and Music by Neil Diamond

1. L. A.'s fine, __ the sun shines most the time,
2. *See additional lyrics*

and the feel - in' is lay back.

Palm trees grow, and rents are low. __ But you know I keep think - in' 'bout __

mak - in' my way back. __

Well,

I'm New York Cit - y born and raised, but now - a - days __ I'm lost be - tween two

shores.   L. A.'s fine, but it ain't home. _

New York's home, but it ain't mine _ no ____ more. _____

Chorus

____ "I am," I said _____ to no one there. _

_____ And no one heard ____ at all, ____ not

e - ven the chair. _____ "I am," I cried. __

_____ "I am," said I. _____

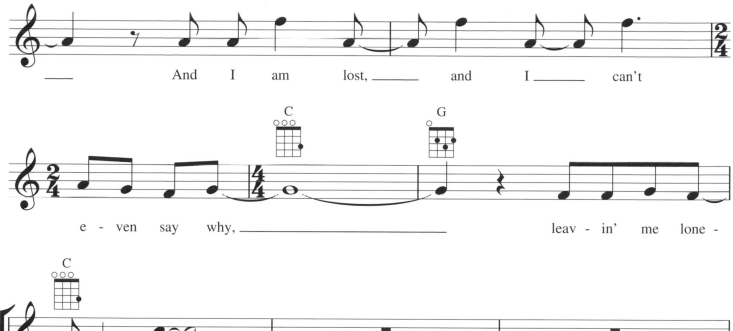

And I am lost, _____ and I _____ can't

e - ven say why, _____ leav - in' me lone -

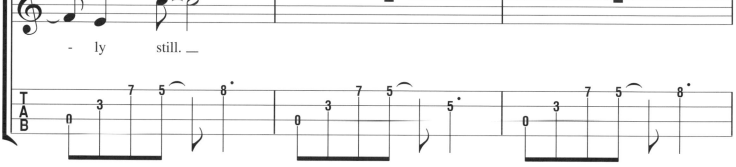

- ly still. __

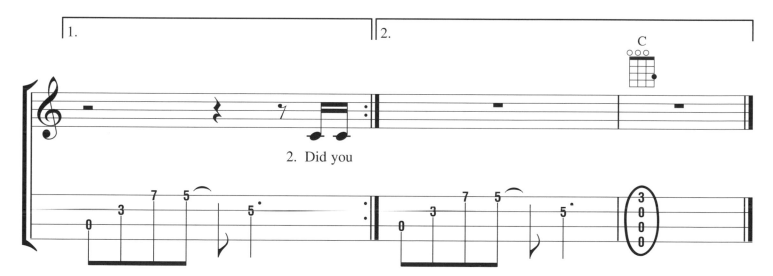

2. Did you

Additional Lyrics

2. Did you ever read about a frog who dreamed
   Of being a king and then became one?
   Well, except for the names and a few other changes,
   If you talk about me, the story's the same one.
   But I got an emptiness deep inside,
   And I've tried, but it won't let me go.
   And I'm not a man who likes to swear,
   But I've never cared for the sound of being alone.
   Chorus

I'm a Believer

Words and Music by Neil Diamond

Chorus

Then I saw her face; _____ now I'm a be- liev-

- er! Not a trace _____ of doubt _ in my

mind. _____ I'm in love, and I'm a be-

To Coda

liev- er! I could-n't leave her if I tried. ____

Interlude

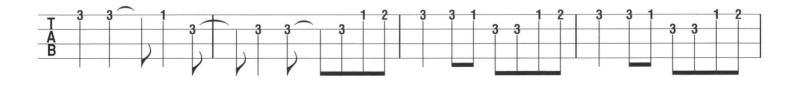

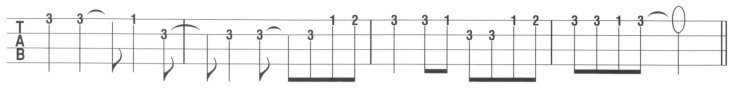

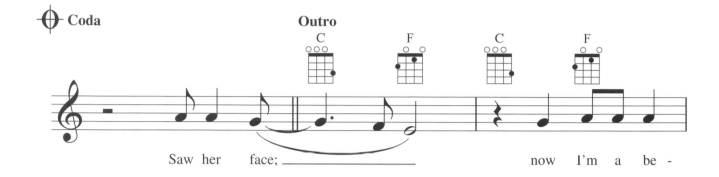

Coda   Outro

Saw her face; _____ now I'm a be -

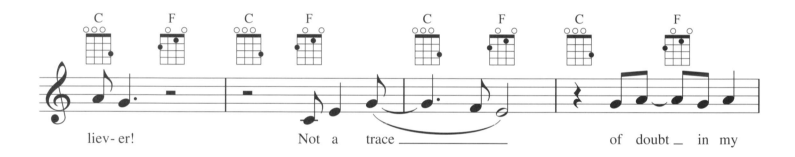

liev- er!   Not a trace _____ of doubt _ in my

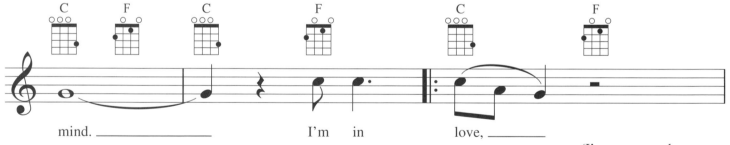

mind. _____   I'm in love, _____ (I'm a be -

Repeat and fade

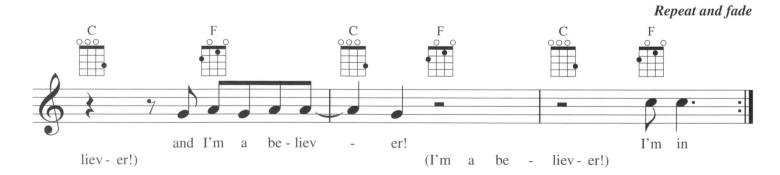

and I'm a be - liev - er!   I'm in
liev- er!)   (I'm a be - liev- er!)

Love on the Rocks

from the Motion Picture THE JAZZ SINGER
Words and Music by Neil Diamond and Gilbert Becaud

now all I want   is a smile.

𝄋 **Chorus**

First they say __ they want __ you,   how they real-ly   need __ you.

Sud-den-ly, you   find __ you're out __ there   walk-ing in a storm.

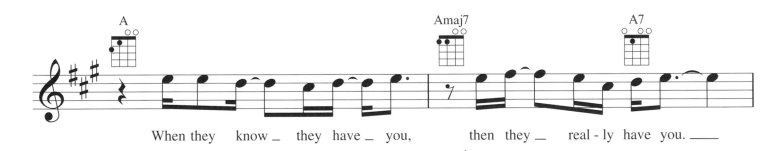

When they   know __ they have __ you,   then they __ real-ly have you. ___

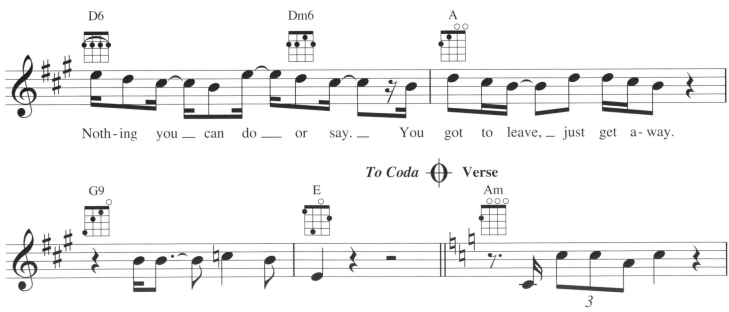

Noth-ing   you __ can do __ or   say. __   You   got   to leave, __ just get a-way.

To Coda ⊕ **Verse**

We all ___ know the   song.   3. You need what you need,

34

you can say what you want. __   Not much you can do   when the

feel-ing is gone.   May be   blue skies a - bove,   but it's

D.S. al Coda

cold   when your love's on   the rocks.

Coda

Outro-Verse

Love on   the rocks   ain't no sur-prise.

Pour me   a   drink, __   and I'll tell you my lies. __   Yes - ter-day's gone,

and now all   I want   is a   smile.

If You Know What I Mean

Words and Music by Neil Diamond

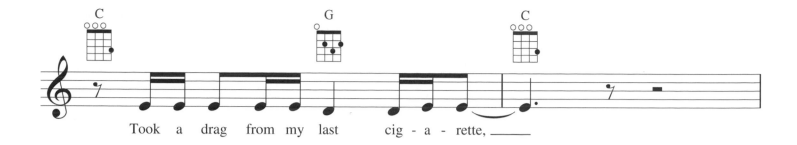

Took a drag from my last cig - a - rette, _____

took a drink from a glass of old _____ wine.

I closed my eyes, and I could make it real and

feel it one more time. _____ Can you

𝄋 Pre-Chorus

hear it, babe? _   Can you hear it, babe? _
hear it, babe? _   Do you hear it, babe? _

From an - oth - er time, ___   from an -
It was an - oth - er time, ___   it was an -

oth - er place, ___   do you re - mem-ber it, babe?
oth - er place. ___   Do you re - mem-ber it, babe?

Chorus

And the ra - di - o played like a car - ni - val

tune as we lay in our bed in the oth - er

room, when we gave it a - way for the sake of a

dream in a pen-ny ar-cade, if you know what I

Verse

Fine

mean. 2. Here's to the songs we used to

sing, and here's to the times we used ___ to know. ___

It's hard to hold them in our arms a - gain but

D.S. al Fine

hard to let them go. ___ Do you

Longfellow Serenade

Words and Music by Neil Diamond

you.   I'll   weave   his   web ___ of   rhyme

up - on   the sum - mer   night. ____   We'll

leave   this   world - ly   time   on   his   wing - ed   flight. ___

Then   come, and   as ___ we   lay   be - side   this sleep - y   glade, _

___   there   I ___ will   sing ___ to   you ___ my   Long - fel - low ser -

1.
- e - nade.

2.
- e - nade. _____

Play Me

Words and Music by Neil Diamond

some - one _____ as though I'd done some - one
trav - el up - on _____ a road that was

wrong some - where, _____ but I don't know where.
thorned and nar - row. _____ An - oth - er place,

I don't know where come
an - oth - er grace would

late - ly.
save me.

Chorus

You are the sun, I am the moon, you are the words,

I am the tune: Play _ me. _

Fine

44

45

Red, Red Wine

Words and Music by Neil Diamond

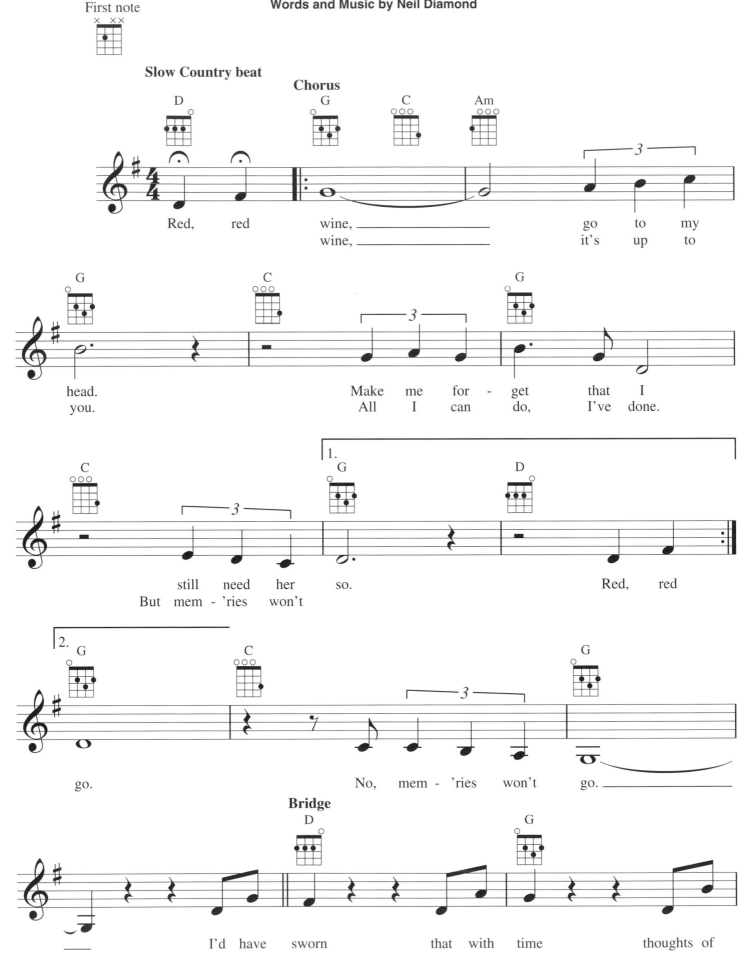

you would leave my head. I was wrong, and I

find just one thing makes me for - get. Red, red ____

Chorus

wine, ____ stay close to me.

Don't let me be a - lone. It's tear-ing a -

part my blue, blue heart. ____

September Morn

Words and Music by Neil Diamond and Gilbert Becaud

day. Two lov - ers play - ing scenes __ from some ro - man - tic play.

Sep - tem - ber morn - ings still can make me feel that

Verse

way. 2. Look at what you've done.

Why, you've be - come a grown - up girl.

I still can hear you cry - ing in the

cor - ner of your room. And look how __ far we've come: so

far   from   where   we   used   to   be,

but   not   so   far   that   we've   for - got - ten

Chorus

how   it   was __ be - fore.   Sep - tem - ber   morn.   Do you re -

mem - ber ___ how we danced __ that night a - way?   Two lov - ers

play - ing scenes __ from some ro - man - tic play.   Sep - tem - ber

morn - ings   still   can   make   me   feel   that   way.

Sweet Caroline

Words and Music by Neil Diamond

Interlude

Outro-Chorus

Sweet Car - o - line, _____ good times

nev - er seemed __ so good.

Sweet Car - o - line, _____ I be - lieve ___

Repeat and fade

__ they nev - er could. __

Shilo

Words and Music by Neil Diamond

1. Young child ___ with dreams, ___ dream - ing ___ each
2. Young girl ___ with fire, ___ some - thing ___ said

dream on ___ your own.
she un - der - stood.

When chil - dren
I want - ed ___ to

play, ___
fly. ___

seems like ___ you end up ___ a -
She made ___ me end feel like ___ I

Pre-Chorus

lone.
could.

Pa - pa says he'd love ___
Held my hand out, and I ___
Had a dream, and it filled ___

___ to be with ___ you ___
___ let her take ___ me, ___
___ me with won - der. ___

if he had the time.
blind as a child.
She had oth - er plans. ___

So you turn to the on - ly friend you can
All I saw was the way that she made me
"Got to go, and I know that you'll un - der -

find,
smile,
stand."

there in your mind.
she made me smile.
I un - der - stand.

Chorus

Shi - lo, when I was young, ___

I used to call your name. ___ When no one else would come, ___

To Coda

Shi - lo, you al - ways came. ___

And we'd
And you'd
Come to -

Coda

D.S. al Coda

1.

play.

2.

stay.

day.

55

Solitary Man

Words and Music by Neil Diamond

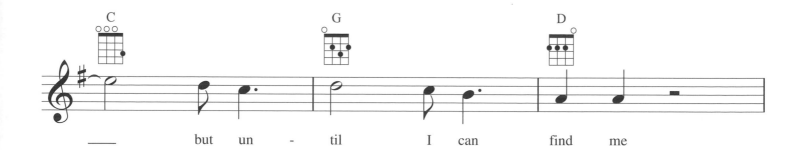

but un - til   I   can   find   me

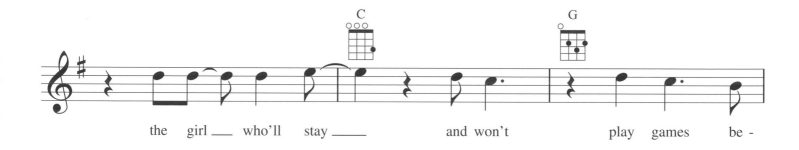

the girl ___ who'll   stay ____   and won't   play games   be -

hind   me,   I'll   be   what   I   am: _____

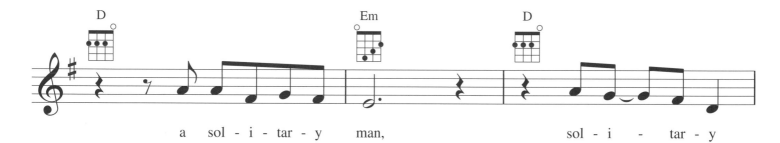

a   sol - i - tar - y   man,   sol - i - tar - y

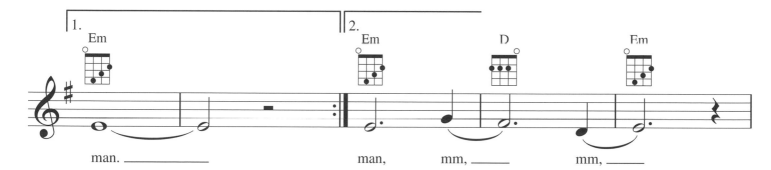

man. _____   man,   mm, _____   mm, _____

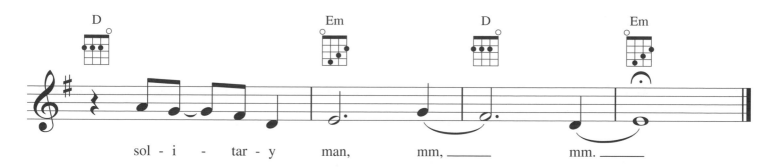

sol - i - tar - y   man,   mm, _____   mm. _____

Song Sung Blue

Words and Music by Neil Diamond

out a - gain. ___ Song sung blue, weep-in' like a

wil - low. Song sung blue, sleep - in' on my

pil - low. Fun - ny thing, ___ but you can sing ___

___ it with a cry in your voice ___

and, be - fore you know it, {get start} to feel - in' good. ___ You sim - ply

got no choice. ___

Yesterday's Songs

Words and Music by Neil Diamond

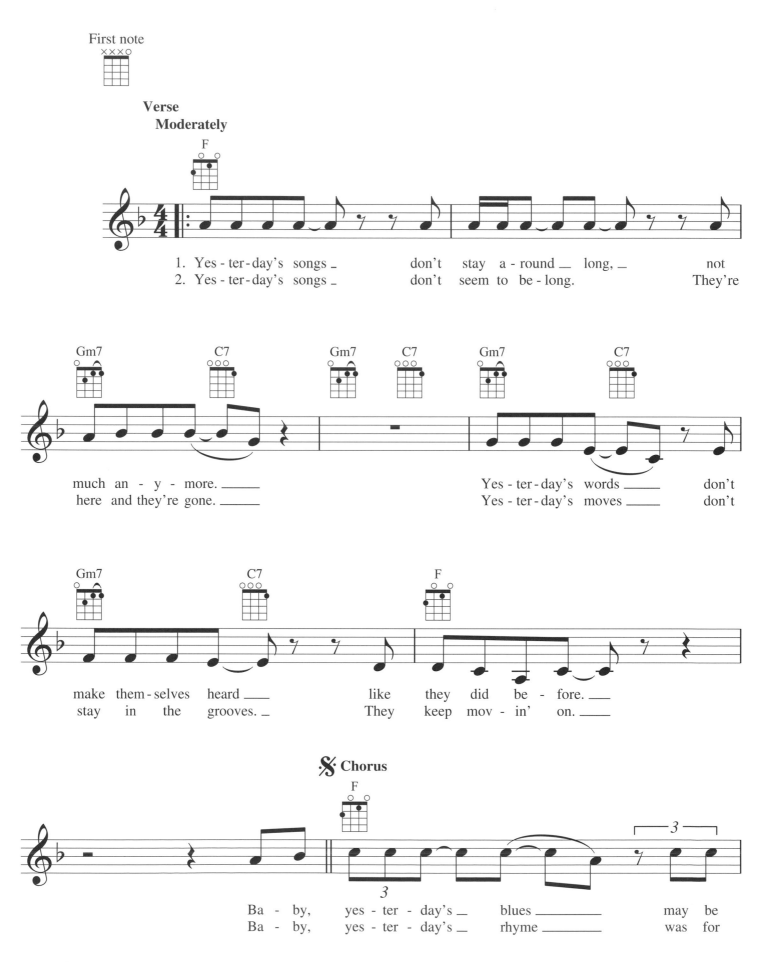

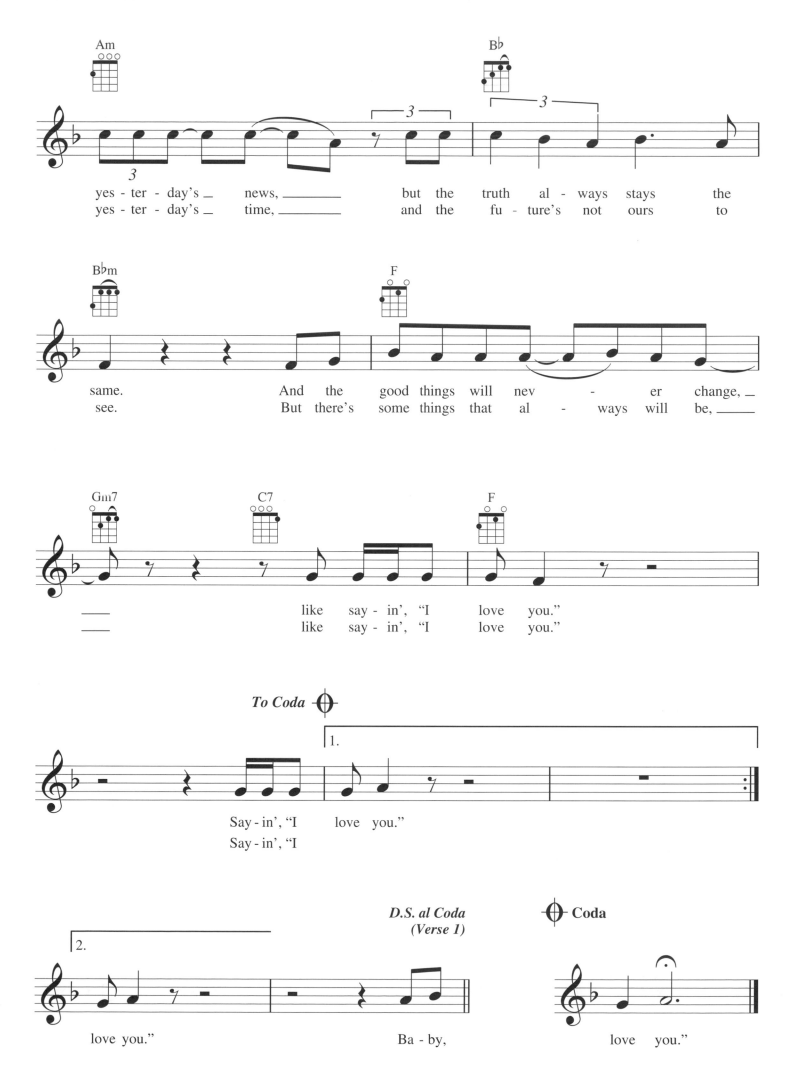

yes - ter - day's _ news, _____ but the truth al - ways stays the
yes - ter - day's _ time, _____ and the fu - ture's not ours to

same. And the good things will nev - er change, _
see. But there's some things that al - ways will be, _____

_____ like say - in', "I love you."
_____ like say - in', "I love you."

To Coda

1.
Say - in', "I love you."
Say - in', "I

2.
love you."

D.S. al Coda
(Verse 1)
Ba - by,

Coda
love you."

You Don't Bring Me Flowers

Words by Neil Diamond, Marilyn Bergman and Alan Bergman
Music by Neil Diamond

late at night   when it's good for you   and you're

feel - in' all right,   well, you just roll o - ver and you

turn out the light.   And you don't bring me flow - ers an - y -

Verse

more.   2. It used to be so nat - 'ral

to talk a - bout for - ev - er,   but used-to-be's don't count an - y - more. _ They just

lay on the floor till we sweep them a - way.   And, ba - by, I re - mem - ber

all the things you taught me: I learned how to laugh, and I learned how to cry. Well, I learned how to love, e - ven learned how to lie. You'd think I could learn how to tell you good - bye 'cause you don't bring me flow - ers an - y - more.

Outro

Well, you'd think I could learn how to tell you good - bye 'cause you don't bring me flow - ers an - y - more.